M E A D

M   E

The University of Georgia Press / Athens and London

A   D

An Epithalamion

Julie Carr

Published by the University of Georgia Press
Athens, Georgia 30602

© 2004 by Julie Carr
The paper in this book meets the guidelines for
permanence and durability of the Committee on
Production Guidelines for Book Longevity of the
Council on Library Resources.

Designed by Tim Roberts
Typeset in 11/13.5 Adobe Garamond and Minion
Printed and bound by Thomson-Shore, Inc.

Printed in the United States of America
08 07 06 05 04 P 5 4 3 2 1

Library of Congress Cataloging-in-Publication Data

Carr, Julie, [date]
Mead : an epithalamion / Julie Carr.
p.   cm.
Includes bibliographical references.
ISBN 0-8203-2684-4 (pbk. : alk. paper)
1. Marriage—Poetry.
2. Love poetry, American.
I. Title.
PS3603.A77425M43 2004
811'.6—dc22

2004007219

British Library Cataloging-in-Publication Data available

for Tim
and for my parents

The Outer—from the Inner
Derives its Magnitude—

Emily Dickinson

Contact is crisis.

Anne Carson

My first thought was "Good God, it's over!"

But it's not. The challenge is now to make certain that it's
not over.

2

Overabundant sun. *It* doesn't want to stop.
It doesn't want to *stop*.

Topology: mere hills
until you're in them, then,

mere road, mere grass.

Memory is itself remembered
as I am not

with my time but behind it.

Still, she's crying in the car and I'm singing to her.
To interpret the singing, she looks at me.

To say, I see you, I open my eyes wider.

Come, my heart or my project,
my loved one or my unlocatable:

you're impairing your vision by holding objects too close,

like the man who ate his own skin,
daily living as self-storage

(trees crowding *that* frame,
sidewalks of cup tops,
mouths sipping description).

Then the rectangular storage container turns out to be
    a city

which might mean stepping over

a permanently ruptured sky.

What can be added here to suggest development?
As story makes way for theme, theme for method.

"Problem: what to do with the body,"
once fed, clothed, put to bed . . .

Like the pages and pages, thousands upon thousands
the philosopher filled in the effort to prove something

could be known because it was invented by its knower.
But a mother argued the point,

coming to refuse the knowing of.

("Actually," wrote the professor, "you could have been a
    little more analytical.")

(When the mother was dancing, she wanted to sleep.
When the mother stopped dancing, she wanted to sleep.)

I read: "The tree like a valve of the heart opens in the
    open sun."

I said: "The tree like a room of voices weighs in at an
    illegible density."

I thought of you as a circle caught within a rectangle

which meant there was space around you but you couldn't
    get to it.

Closer observation revealed:
the empty glass reflecting waves of light:

a shore where one can rest, one can rest endlessly in a glut
    of belonging.

Everywhere, one face.

You, rolling sand into wheels.

Sex, an impossibility the universe grew out of.

THE INSIDE OBSERVED
BY THE OUTSIDE

If even one's closest friends are unknowing, if for everyone there is
only *black mantle*, the unrevealed, a kind of tepid mood results,
like drying cement, staying too long in the shower, speaking
English in non-English-speaking countries, laughing in the tracks
of "to laugh," struggling to get the kids out of the house, *Ja*—you
suffer. Dread pink. Spread before the poem, flattened by the desire
to be penetrated by its plan. And when nothing happens, turning
to sleep as an alternative. Or, to put it more boldly:

I'm sleeping *in* the dance that I'm currently dreaming and you, of
course, are watching me, which is how I, evidently, desire you.
The dance I am improvising is inspired by the approach of your
vision. Fellow eyes, blending the dance. Tulip skirt. Rose lift.
Mirrored, moved, dove. The diagonal dive. Sore and

time-wrapped
like sand (if waves can be said to *be* time, which certainly they
    can, they're so

metronominal).

Awake: kids jump pools, this rising tide of

4

Terror, and the tree breaks.

That bird's a singer and I'm nothing
if not poised to listen, but I miss

the song entirely and only catch the breathing

sounds. What

did *you* mean when you said "attack"?

    Having one certainly distinguishes itself from
      making one.

Writing is conjure. It's trying but true.
This is a dragon cave,

out there's a whale. A real mean one, Honey-bun.

    Up here's a trail. As she tires

I tighten the straps that hold her.
So much for security—

a flash of falling through the tree's eye.

"Matter gave birth to passion," as in:

"What is the matter?"

"Nothing."

"You look like you're going to cry."

"I am. I am."

5

Pulled off the face. Not wanting to be found replaceable, not
wanting, in this life, to be found replacing, they turned sweet
rooms to dirty rooms. There was time and there was timing. Then
children beat all. The disciplined pen saying, expose:
"the enclasping flow." Expose: laughter,

this loose knot.

She walks off and wants to return and returns and wants to leave.
She walks off, not giving up anything. Returns with another hand.
Come to the party. Lips. Screens. Pulsing light. Come into the
party. Lips, screens, pulsing light.

A tree can be full of flowers. Differently, a cup can be full of tea.

Elsewise, the human, full of only itself,
feels empty.

DOING

I rode up the hill to change my words and found a shadow sharp as ink. I sat on a bench named Anna until a ball came rolling under. Then I knelt. Sun goes low and shadows sharper. I sit on a bench with a girl's name. A father and a son play ball. After we got to this road, this garden, we bought some things and others we ate.

I rode up the hill to change my time and found my face was lying. I want the same thing as the sun. I sit on a bench with a girl's face until a ball comes rolling under. And I feel. Some play ball and some go down. After we sat we gardened. *Dad?* Others we left behind.

I slept up the hill to change my name, my name I found in the sun. A father went down, another went under. My face was a garden until I woke to Anna. Anna. We found some time; sleep, we left behind.

I ate the hill. I ate the garden. My face was sun, I slept. A father played, a son rolled over, a bench, my sister, Anna. I benched until I knelt, I said, the shadow sharpens my name. Late in the garden—

7

at six playing lion-
mommy and blowing the head off

a flower, swimming

in a fountain—it didn't seem dirty
like it does now we're making love and I'm thinking

of paying the midwife for delivering the baby,
which means writing a check

then just waiting
to see what happens to the bank account,

a kind of reverse sex if sex is depositing something
and then waiting to see what happens to the family.

And the interest of sex is a body. The interest of a body is
    filth and food.

As what interests the eye is light, of course,

while light in the eye means the eye is either loving
or wet—

THE OUTSIDE DEMANDS;
THE INSIDE DELIVERS

What is "pushing"

Pushing is the last part, but altogether the most active. It is a forest and sweltering path of fission. A separation and a cooling. It is a bullish measure, a lock-headed argument, a lid and also a bottom.

What is "measure"

Measure is flickering on the wrist of a fallen woman. It's a promise led on a leash to a watering hole; it is drooling, it drawls out its presentiments, it promises to dance with the lick of flame it will extinguish. It promises to rise up and meet. Measure becomes direction, determined. Its function being to conjoin and so dissolve opposing forces. Love, I am coming.

What is "paradox"

A bad one and a good one. One that punctures, another that spreads. Love, I am here is a paradox, for love demands direction but refuses arrival. Juliet's second line dismantled by the play's conclusion. Spreading her fingers, between them, sky. "Quickly!" I heard, and turned.

What is a "man"

Servant. A tangle told with eyes (they deposit bits of seeing on the objects in front). A sun, a hand on the table with a red flower blooming out of its thumb. Not an arm, not a leg, nor any other part belonging to. Servant, but itself observed as generating. Hush, said the man to the baby, I've told you already, I am speaking now.

When we returned from the play I went to bed and began to read my book. I read on and on until I reached the end, and found after that I could not sleep. A field of white persisted in my mind, yet each time I began to walk its length in search of some defining edge, I found none was possible. There was no way to cease what I had begun.

HOW THE INSIDE BECOMES
THE OUTSIDE

      The weakness sings.
Matter falls to
fill itself, its own
song not yet
sounding, but
its comedy pulsing
through the very hour,
through the body,
that contains it.

      Inception means
that like a spider
hung in its belly's
creation,
a future tense clings
inside the present
and becoming it
destroys it.

      The daughter lay down
as soon as she had
weight;
she could feel
and asked to be
increased.

　　　　Falling
to pieces,
the mother moved
into what moved
out of what
she was made.

Syllables for lips:
Melon drama skidding red.

I think. Mouse thinks. Happiness in
her hand.

Her face, slick fur, hovers.

Listens. More dearth. Sad face. Like looking
into one's own

windows

where an unidentifiable
purse

is spilled throughout
three rooms,

where the unborn
enervate, show how

lying will
make a mistake.

If I say "she" that's one person.
If I say "he" that's another.
And the one who says "I" is the one with the most to hide.

She lifts up her walker and walks across the street.
He zips up his leather tight as an orange peel.
I put my tongue to the button.

One kind of want is the kind that breaks worlds apart.
Another kind rests its hands on its knees.
A third avoids the child. Or coddles it.

THE OUTSIDE OVERHEARD
BY THE OUTSIDER

Citing tensions as advice, four more Americans in Vienna.
   I was alone

when my husband surprised me with two children;
whose is the void from which the stars are cast?

Waking in fog, the great neutralizer, I plan my next
   thought in prose, my self in debt.

I am halved, housed; roused
I am haved,

am that which is counted,
twice and twice again.

Leaves fracture the shape of a tree;
what loving is.

Two eggs boil; my children are not home—
moving, measured,

assured. When I hear
a voice I assume it's my son's,

when not, I have
the sum of my arms.

14

The blue glass object remembered as in a window but delayed. As wheels or what glows. Absolutely, the flower girl spoke, she was on her bike, her back to us. Pollen her hands, her pedals flair. A scarlet alphabet across the sky read: where is safety? enter *there*.

THE INSIDE OF THE INSIDE EXPOSED

And the wild pigs pop the cooler top—smart snouts—
while she, wed, spoons in spills. Sun makes

the day, though "over there" means
there's a flip side to this.

When "nothing" stands for:
"I'm angry," and silence for:

"Your speech is too mannered, too sure of its own style,
    and this bothers me because, like all attempts to avoid
    disclosure, it fails to hide your shame,"

then silence returned means:

taste it? I mean

the salt, and

      salt-made men.

16

Dark wet town we roll through, four, the horn.

Tree! She says with a finger extended, some hoops torn.

My love eating ice makes a crease in his memory to forgive me,
   laughter.

When mothers are funny the children are baffled, later,
   embarrassed, three chairs.

Fault I took in my mouth like a train goes into the night,
   the ocean.

THE OUTSIDE DEMANDS;
THE INSIDE DELIVERS

What is a "name"

A name is reserved. The body of water had a wall around it, a wall
of signs. Nonetheless we went in, slid off the neck of the beast,
burdened paradoxically, to push. We went into the name of the
thing and there swam and drank. I was finally balanced on a rock,
and finally, doffed mine & took thine.

What is "black mantle"

We are familiar. A balanced economy. We prattle or encounter a
tale. We are familiar with the rank of night (civil night). Slipping
on a debt, we invest and are enclosed in an embattled city. The
black mantle is first and foremost a window and a shroud. They've
exchanged you and you and returned themselves and you're given
a special tree-gift, which they toss in order to save.

What is "nurse"

The greatness of these sometimes contradicts the future.
Contractions return us to the present (her airy tongue). This
account always infinite, cyclical, eternal. Return and on it they
empty their terrible hunger. Return and in their voice you're
ay, ay, ay. On her back she falls. There, still.

What is the "time"

His name might be moving across a field somewhere to the beat
booming from the ocean's pass, pass, pass. His name, says this
chapter, need not be known. Bondage is a horse and may not
speak aloud. Instead: I am a sentence and you a note held.
Pocketed, and so stuck in the wandering. Time pours out of my
breast when I sleep. Time-wrapped my rest is a field now advanc-
ing, now remembered. Nowhere appearing to rise up and meet,
dissolves again. The rest is here.

FIVE SENTENCES WITH VERBS

In a photograph we stand, my son on my hip, swallow.

Our remarried parents tilt under the pressure of sodden words, spill.

Once when a mossy stone gleamed beneath her foot, my sister, pausing, is.

He steadies a hand that trembles to touch the girl's glowing belly, thinking.

On this channel we have birds floating, wings folded, and swimmers undressing; it snows.

Believe me, the night was dreamless.
Rising to go to one, then the other—

Finally, the bird,
a blessing. No reflections
anywhere.

Compliments from the old to the young.
The Hello Kitty bag dirty, open.
Being is examined in the phenomenological study
of the gospels, but is badly translated
and the translator overpaid. There are three kinds
of business (this from the Buddhist on tape): mine,
yours, and God's. Discomfort arises
when I'm in yours, you're in mine, or we're in
God's. This is an interesting idea,
but I'm nursing my baby. It'd be difficult to say
whose business the milk is.
"The self is a servant only
to its source." I watched the jay's tail
beat the rhythm of its singing
in the plum tree. Meredith's sure
a monkey bit a plum, and looks for a fallen
half-gone one.

Every morning the woman with the walker
lifts it up so she can walk
more freely, like a woman from another century
might have lifted the hem of her skirt,

or like the characters in an Austen novel
descending smoothly into marriage,
all impediments
revealed as false
or temporary,
as marriage, like death, takes even

those who mock it.

THE OUTSIDE OBSERVED
BY THE INSIDE

I rolled up my window. AM radio. Plugged my nose.
Then, he stopped his car and said, "go ahead and hit me."
Someone's head was out on the front lawn. Danny was all
talk, but then *you* had to get out there. But now he's
arrested and it serves him right, riding up and down my
block on a bicycle. I tried scaring him away. Then one day
I heard shooting inside my garage. What a scene at that
house. Lotta negative energy. But nobody deserves to have
their jaw broken.

I'm talking
frying pans—

(those domestic
paragraphs)

THE INTERIOR BLENDS WITH
THE INSIDE

—as a nine-year-old boy stuck in the dinosaur stage,
as a T-shirt with a flat map beneath,
as a nine-year-old fuck-forever on the dim-lit stage—

the interior of the dream like a clothing store
designed to stroke the customer's
self-esteem.

ARROW

I dream you are a cat named Arrow.
I dream you are a cat named Are.

Open the door and let the wind come home.
Open the door and come home.

I dream you are a door, an arrow.
I dream you are a door; you are.

Open the name and let the dream come in.
Open the name and let.

I name the door; then the cat comes in.
I name the door, then the cat.

The cat is a door. The cat, the wind.
The arrow opens up the wind.

A cat is a dream; a cat is asleep.
You dream I sleep; you spin in a dream.

A door is a name. A name is a door.
I pin the wind to the door and sleep.

ARROW

Dream you are a cat named Arrow
Open the door let the wind come in
Read you rare O take my worry
Pen the road Tell the now home no
Dire hour air of ache I'm worn
Not this dare Let this new omen out
Arid house fair soft chair am yours
Win this riot lest the web seem torn
Rid your fire for char makes sore
Own that road later The severed names tear
Dreamt you were a cat named Rouse
Open the door until the veer assumes right

Smell of onion. Or perhaps just "onion." (A bit of research and off we go.) A fountain designed first of all for bathing, only later this didn't seem sanitary. A fountain into which I pour my face. Not unlike a tired child sipping milk through a straw. Or two-year-old Jesse wandering freely into the street. Eggplant on an oily plate. I walk in, having walked out. Do you think it possible to dream the same dream 365 nights in a row? I wake in a rising and a clearing of fog. Fans do that. Fans and belts. Poems volt and an idea can turn sour like milk, a swimmer at her wall. The model pivots in her chair. Travelers, waves, the moon. A mood. Centrifugal. A drummer's hands: the kind of spin that doesn't spin out. Leaves turn and children turn out, as do the dancer's feet. Hair turns and "one lived with the portrait of the other." Liking or not liking a book, one reads not for the author's voice, but for one's own.

YOU

may think you're addressed—
may think a reader like a neighbor for whom we undress

but whose eyes we
never meet.

You may think

I do this for you, and are you
flattered?

But it's a burden

to behold
one's neighbors theatrically

lit and it's a burden to be beheld.
                                        You

may think yourself a god
from whom the poem begs

an audience or you may,

like an actor

becoming your attire

stand up on the gaudy

stage I've made, waiting to be prompted
into speech.

        But I

can never tell
who you are.

WHAT IS "TO TELL"

Telling fell when the water did. It fell in broken bits and we watched it pretend toward whole. The bare backs of his legs, first on foot, then the other. I was extended or shaking, shook. The teller's mouth met the objects of her tale as red ink to the flower it becomes. And falling meant there was somewhere we were to be going.

The rubber ladder, the receding ladder, the ladder of light, the ladder without rungs, the latter ladder, the lead, the late, the laughing ladder.

THREE SENTENCES WITH ADVERBS

The pool was empty but for my husband, and he, not really a swimmer, floated around calmly, happily.

Rain becoming snow as the train passes into afternoon becoming evening, gradually, suddenly.

He asked for an interpretation of his dream and I declined; the answer was in the silence, obviously.

EPITHALAMION:
SPENSER (ECHO RING)

You learned early water to lament.

           Now lie early before.

The woods may, all the woods,

           the woods shall.

A lamp, the world's lamp,

           bring with you bring

nymphs the discolored mead

           to diaper.

Wake now. My love now

           is hark. How shrill, how dance

how ravish

           quite?

Tell me, did you? But if you

           open the

behold

           while now all is done,

the woods, all the woods,

           the woods.

Bring home.

Bring

home-restraint,

Pour out,

Now all ring you ah

home-sweat,

home-stay.

pour not, pour out.

when.

Now cease.

Now day,

Let no, no let,

who is (calm, quiet,

Now welcome.

now night.

but let

nor treason,

nor false).

Bound, enlarged

as might.

Bouncing her on my lap—

    of course the pen is the better toy.

Smiley faces in burnt crops or on mailboxes,

    which is the better idea? Or rather,

in the bread? The dog? The sun

    hits the light and reflection dulls the glass.

I dream a child is sick while beside me my husband

    dreams a suicide. The therapist asks

what we want out of therapy.

    We laugh. Unfortunately

we don't know. The lake is dark—

    just like the unknown—

but that wasn't how I meant it. Rather,

(You get out—go, go, go.)

Wanting happiness we imagine

separately.

The object loses ground when what I'll call here "external path"
becomes *into*, becomes the voice of spirit that heats heat—swollen into
maternal causes, face upon face rising out of the

FIRE

When he comes home I'm in the bedroom with the baby
    and our son is watching *Barney.*
    On the table bathed in tomato and onion is the fish
    he cleaned the night before by dripping its blood
    into the sink.

Quickly we eat, then quickly I am back upstairs to read:
    Mrs. Ramsay's death, Lily Briscoe's need to paint,
    Mr. Ramsay's gorgeous self-pity. And the baby
    sleeps fitfully. I know she will wake.

The next morning I wash all the windows inside and out
    while she watches me from the stroller. Pollen,
    dust, black ink from the newspaper on my hands.

THREE PARTS BROKEN FOR BLEND

Lash or lip—gray like the marbled or mired wave-wiped
stone.

I don't. But you know your "must"
is wrapped in mammalian
feeling
like or likened to
a door.

—

A barrier leans on an advertisement.
Whether the rim of my cup is

soft or firm decides me
and I stand.
Thirsty?
I ask, when the
tree.

—

Usually to dream of dancing meant
I'd left something undone—

mistaking the passing of
bodies for that.
Your eye, the remaining
horror-joke—
partial.

WATER / FIRE (FOR THE BABY)

You, a net for eyes—little fish—
  lost in a quarter inch of water.

  Like flame softens wax
    the spills make
    your colors bleed.

The ordinary heft of
  a leg over another leg
  is evidence that

          the net is tight,
          my gaze given.

  By noon the house
  floats up—

        a spark
        in the draft of the burning.

DOING

Freeway wraps. Fog lifts. Traffic bleats. They are looking

for something to talk about. Luckily the baby moves and
they watch her. The boy wants a video.

The neighbors cry through the windows. The baby must
suck herself to sleep. Like a cinder, sunset bursts—

Must we

continue the conversation? as she closes the door.

34

Weeping into the weather—a cold summer day. *Cause?* Upstairs she moves around in bed. That's it, the end to my solitude. I want, briefly, to die. *Effect!* Then there's the blue bead, an airplane overhead. These things do not make me want to stay alive. I want to stay alive because the baby needs me. I want to die because the baby needs me.

Image: a tapestry woven of rusted metal scraps and bits of cotton waste. It is at once delicate and obtrusive, at once dead and alive.

Blend: this tapestry with the dream: leaping from a balcony— falling so slowly that falling becomes flight.

Her voice enters my body like a mechanical arm, forcing me to stand. Rust is the mouth and genitals. Cotton, the eyes and ears.

Now we must create some distance, and distance looks like this:

> A hand flat as a pane of glass moves gradually forward, palm out, as if to slap, as if to become
>
> ironic. Text. A screen.

BLEND

This is my window. Just now
I have so softly wakened,
I thought that I would float.

    My skin is cherry juice, her mouth around my finger—
    star—the cherry juice under her

I could think that everything
was still me all around;
transparent as a crystal's

    lip. Out, wind. But I asked for the wind. I asked for these
    clouds as

depths, darkened, mute.

    boundary: Now she's sucking my shoulder. The animal's hide.
    But that squirrel's coming into the house. Mild shock:
    Out, out!

How far does my life reach,
and where does the night begin?

The leaf is a border. The color green, a wall.
When the walls become vials,
drink.

But darkness whaling in.
　Won't and wouldn't make.
　　Swimming with vision loosed on the grass.
　　　Begin and cease and then again begin.

Ah edges drear.
　Will move my arm.
　　Slap charge across space.
　　　Echo thrown, echo bound.

Nor chair nor rest.
　Nor exactitude nor tact.
　　Bound to unwrap.
　　　Nor stand.

37

THE INSIDE AND THE OUTSIDE
TAKE HANDS

Imagine you were forced to wear a mechanism that
projected all of your thoughts in a fifty-yard radius
around you. After a while, you'd forget to be ashamed.

Perhaps this is already happening.

Are you? he begins—

THE OUTSIDE OBSERVED
BY THE OUTSIDE

"You are the only one for me," he says,
responding to my request for kinder words. The man
driving the car to our left resembles my favorite poet.
I look away before he turns his head.

SIX SENTENCES WITH
AND WITHOUT ADJECTIVES
(PORTRAITS IN BOXES)

Opening an envelope while riding a train, a man with crossed
knees, crying.

Photographs of dollar bills enlarged beyond recognition become
metaphors for rain.

We learned finally that manufacturing complexities was effective
and therefore to be avoided.

Slowly a person is "diminished," says my mother; she can see that
I don't "get it," but I am her "best friend" anyway.

I was alone in the pool but for a man who did not swim, but
rather sank to the bottom where he walked in slow circles
with his hands on his hips while seeming to speak.

Each time he drew an eye he named it either a sun-eye or a moon-
eye, the difference being in the lashes.

DEFINITE / INDEFINITE

                             a
                      the   a
      the   a mouth
     the mouth   a moment
   the word   a
                  word
the day
                 a word
                 the
                   a
                     the face
                a day
              the child
              a child
             the moment
                                  a
                the
              a hole
              the lack
              a law
  the   law
              a law
             the question
               a
              the
             a mother
              family
             a family
             the touch
               a
  face   a
    the hole   a lack
      the mother   a mother
              the

41

First she looked in the mirror. Then she thought about it. Empty
trees and their dwarfed doubles in the lake. Precisely. Being first
a bird, then a bug, later the woman's legs folded beneath her.

The pride of the parent is painful because it keeps shutting like a
door on springs with each stutter in the child's performance.
He's learning his letters. (bang!) Say, "please." Say, "juice."
(bang! slam!)

But here's a seam, gently torn, and soon there is no word, no
listening ear. And the woman, she's standing now at the edge of
the lake where yesterday a fourteen-year-old drowned when the
lifeguard took a shower. But she knew how to swim. We can't,
by looking or looking again, settle it.

WATER

doesn't break observed my son at Yellowstone Falls. Or it only does, doesn't mend. Kick, I later instruct, my hands around his waist. Mothers eye each other's hips while occasional fathers hoot and caution. I am kind, determined. Or so I strain to seem.

43

We've rented a movie. At first it seems to be about war, which
shames us. Then we realize it's about the-longing-for-home, which
bores us. I build a house and he builds a house and we place the
houses side by side so their windows look into each other. The
houses are small, as if for birds, and fragile, as if of plywood.

Snow, the missing element,

   would fill a hole
           slowly.

HOW HE STANDS, CLOSE ENOUGH

I was am and now in won't but while making am
am nowhere toward.

Sleeping or waking in am not so, would walk in
darkness but.

Won't or wooden and roofed for saw in nodding
in what was.

Won, my sigh was here toward sleep in his door
I was his door.

I ran was light, saw skin become light, plaster or
upholstery, stored face.

I saw in my wasn't but while hair or lip or peeling saw
hill while came.

Am am mama ne'er one draw hill coming mama
worn out drawn.

Peeling or calling in my tone is.

Do road do den calm now strait or dour wonder
what danced for.

Now I'm is I signed what saw. Now I'm his ergo
his drought please.

Near near I saw kiss saw tile saw ink became red slap
for hole. You're safe.

Was I in not rail nor pill nor lapping was lie my Mecca.

Will was or will is will to enisle the yes! say or warn yes
where worried.

To continue to lack lapping in darkness
but eternal note's.

Won't win would do in for under done can own more.

Washed eye not run lips sleep up in my shore
mortal or am ache.

Come the window the moon lies the tide is now we
here we here.

FOURTH PART BROKEN

For one block   I often misstep
I remove my   in just this way
and my hand   lunging to avoid
                           a rut or a fissure
                           then re-righting myself
                           in the wake of a
                           memory
I am unable   so that a new
                           clean mind
                           comes up vertical
                           with the familiar
                           resolution to hold
to enter she   steady and true just
cries at the door   then a bounding
                           animal

Slipped on the broom's trail, a frenetic shove into fealty. A love of reassurance feeds on, showing all mistakes passable. Our radio protects stark sentences, locked as they are in mouths poised as listening. Our radio softens the ground while roaming. He tampers a recent irrefutable statement: "Angles equal to each other, paired with vertical bars like red ants escaping mark where danger ends." That we remain couched, more unsure, toned like corps dancers framing an erotic leg in blessed fourth position, means our faces are veiled by repetition of form. The leg, a segment only, spins like a moral
or a flame.

FIVE PORTRAITS IN RINGS
(SENTENCES WITH OBJECTS)

Once the stems were plunged into the held-vase, the thought-stream, several standing questions, loosed from the arm, tumbled down.

Every time he spoke we yelled over him in outrage, but his voice nonetheless became the fluid in our throats.

Carrying a hat into the house, throwing it Frisbee-style across the room with a gleeful shout, then a "*What?*"

He claims that the book is about being miserable, but in fact the swimmers were happy, though cold.

Slaying the dragon was not his goal; rather it was to join the dragon and sword into one living being through which he could *see* as she saw through her fingers when hiding her face in her hands.

THE INSIDE ASSERTS ITSELF
ONCE MORE (DREAM #9)

My husband and I are throwing a good-bye party for ourselves in
our old apartment. I've invited Taffy and Don and some other
people, including my X, Y. Y has said he's coming, has sent a
check for $212 to pay for his portion of the food, and has printed
onto the check "Kiss me passionately," and something else I can't
make sense of, though I think it includes the word "heart." I real-
ize on the morning of the party that my husband doesn't know
I've invited Y, that it was a mistake to, and that I must keep him
from coming. The party has two components: a 10:15 brunch and
a four o'clock tea. I think of simply disconnecting the buzzer to
our apartment once all the other guests have arrived, but that
would assume Y to be last. And also, he might call. I think of
unplugging our phone, but it doesn't seem practical. So I decide to
call him, though it's very early, and I will have to wake him. And
then it becomes a task—how to get out of the house to do this.
The party, meanwhile, is starting. People are arriving, and a crew
of other people is behind a counter cooking eggs to everyone's
order. The main chef has his back to me, but I become aware that
I am nevertheless attracted to him, to his arms as he turns the
eggs, and to his voice because he is singing. At least I think he's
singing until someone turns the radio off. Taffy and Don are early
to the party, and following Don's lead, I order a three-egg omelet,
no potatoes, from the attractive chef. Another chef removes a very
large tray of muffins from an oven. I decline, though my husband
is happy—

THE OUTSIDE LAMENTED BY THE INSIDE

The documented body is now freely distorted:
elongated legs, expanded chest,

testicles tucked back against perineum:

deformity as an emblem for history—
the body's own history—being born.

A bird at the window.
Am I sure about that?

The nursery school teacher hasn't heard of *Toy Story* or
Toy Story II,

which is a bit of a put-on, a bit of an affront.
Education as mere witness or "support,"

but what if the child wants to play at killing?
The child wants to play at killing—

these somatic devotions—
(this last thought unclothed).

"But *why* do you want it," asks the sincere mother of the
girl before the Barbies,

"no, just *why?* What is it about it that makes you *want* it?"

Nothing. Just,
wive her.

SIX SENTENCES DARKLY
WITH NOUNS SPENT

My darling ate not, she was planning a coin toss, the lawn became
    pleasure, she gave lip.

A face at the glass when whipping cream was the boy they say
    disturbed of, eating white food, turning.

Once a heron in the lot stood as we prepared to walk, the pond
    rose, gladly, a dog.

No rain, only my mother checking her watch on the train, I fear
    she will be lost, the doors close, I turn to the steps,
    Henry James.

Five years after we married we married, an airplane at dawn
    behind stripped birches, the year ends and yes.

Now day, when day, day light, come day, again day, if day, where
    is the.

51

Down in a torn house I'm holding the boy's hand, the hand
    testing pleasure becomes cup.

Pass the shark, pass the mask, the batter, some more please—I am
    safe, said the boy, taking cream to be home, then window, then
    cream.

If the heavy step of the woman with the stick were to startle you,
    you would turn toward her, glancing on your way the ducks.

Here is where the tracks V the book is cracked a page loosens.

We are born into.

Yes at dawn we married behind branches, for five years after,
    perched, airborne, and.

WHAT IS "TO FALL"

In or out. The birds as a piece or all of one. Lift to fall there and
then the air becomes a shape. Laughter and her knees gave out.
You always joyful in the solemnity of your dance had to carry my
teacher his wife stern on the floor with a brush washed the color
out of the wood and at the same time her hair became clean down
her back the water.

SUBPLOT 4

She traced her foot with a stick in the sand, then refused to step out of
the mark she'd made. "The dunes will decay without us," she said,
afraid of discovering a couple lying in what they thought was a hidden
depression.

(But what *was* it she carried in that plastic bag? It might have been a
rosebush, but it was much too light, seemed to weigh next to nothing,
so perhaps was a paper rosebush . . .)

70

TELLER

Let's go on a walk, spoke the surrounding
luminous flowers.

He lay down on the grass and refused to get up. I was not
    below bribing him with toys and cake.

It was my intention to maintain composure
while insisting on my right to dominate. Badly

I wanted to please each member of my family and at the
    same time wrap

my empty space with space. But here I

stop, for a war has erupted

between the one who tells and the one who bathes.
The teller is impatient and her impatience feeds her

obsessive love of order. The bather, however,
is refusing to get out of the water,

refusing to do any next thing. The bather

is sitting on the drain,
under her lip, nails of tangerine, she's

never naked because of the hair she's not combing,
    hanging her wrist over the edge of the tub, speaking

not a word.

And the teller demands
an imminent death

or a marriage. She feigns
patience, gazing out the window, but she's seeing

red. Lord, the vines do cling, is what she says, but
let her but begin, and she'll begin to make an end,

string in her mouth unwinding.

Someone must die, is what she's thinking,
let's make a choice, make a choice, a choice—

for she knows, she's been taught, that rhythm is a
    powerful component of a tale.

The bather meanwhile has been drinking
the bathwater, and she leaks now salt

from her skin and eyes. Taste her, she's coded,
she means, as a metaphor, to be explained.

Passive, responsive, this hour upon the

drain. This salted

lip, this bit

of . . .

(The teller has given over, she's falling asleep, her cheek to
   the . . .)

EPITHALAMION: HOPKINS

Head
a name   a "key word"

contents   persistent client state

                          (body)

width 24
height 68   the text

press   help

        parent-self status

——

Go to the

name   name

        O where what can

Name   There again!
weedio weedio   so tiny a trickle

                                              and all around not to be found

Well, after all!   (all but Hark!)
I am the little   dlark

—

Round a ring   around a ring
and while I sail   (must listen)
the skylark is my   cousin

And we   a name
within

—

Very glad

      O very glad

the ear in milk   )

    tatter dainty head

—

Man the jack is   his mate a
hussy

   my mate bearing my rock

Hearer hear o   what I do

we are leaf   branchy bushy

loins of   hill (gluegold)

75

we are there   hear a shout
in the cover   boys from the town
bathing

the bevy of them how the boys

—

Here he

he looks about him   swims & swims

Enough now since the

sacred matter that I

mean   (wedlock)
what the water   (spousal love)
names

round the bower is

&&&&&

—

All day long I
fountain flow

parent-self status

Return   thy stress on my being

Help me sir
thou art   man-mate

a target   (a name)

glassy grassy
kind-cold

and on.

55

The bather
is involved in futility. She rolls sand
into wheels and folds sheets of wind. She
pours milk into labyrinthine molds, she does not
stand, her limbs wander without intention, water
widens her skin, her other organs of perception may close.
Birds flood her room, and in this instance, they are without
beak and claw, they are all wing. With them they have brought
their favored environment: ethereal trees, uprooted, trunks and
branches intertwining into vaginal passages the birds thread.
Decisions, the bather long ago decided, are not made but rather
reflected upon after. This attitude is one of supination. This atti-
tude turns slower than the earth and so appears to actually
move backwards. You may yell through the window of this
room, but wings, especially of birds without landing
apparatus, swell sonically and so will drown your
cries. For in this forest of trees spread like legs
and wings rising like water, the bather is
in her element and can afford
little affection.

AIR

If the crow sits on the skull of a deer

that's the

end.

The room is not human and does

not listen.

Marriage lies

on the couch like a flag,

a downed fence,

or alphabet falling

out of correspondence.

We will eat

all that we own,

even the smallest bud.

The monarch clings

to the spokes of the wheel.

Our hands cautious,

we take

its picture.

THE INSIDE LAMENTED
BY THE OUTSIDE (DREAM #10)

The dream of my favorite poet begins with his hand running through his hair. It is a large hand and reminds me of a ping-pong paddle from my grandmother's basement—as if, like that, it is seldom held. The action of combing it through his hair tickles his scalp, but his fingers are numb. How do I know this? Clearly in this dream the border between my favorite poet and myself, though wide, is permeable. I can feel just what he feels though I am sitting in a chair across the room. And then I turn to a mirror that hangs on the wall beside him. And I watch, not him now, but his reflection. He, following my eyes, sees himself too, and shocked by what he sees, exclaims, "I'm so gray!" then shakes his head a little—sad, bewildered. It is, I believe, my job to cheer him up, so I turn the conversation to his poetry. I have many intelligent things to say, and it is evident that he is delighted with my commentary. I, of course, hope this means we will sleep together. But just then I open one of his books and turn to my favorite passage. And now the entire dream is made up of these words—a cluster of lines at the bottom of a page—and the I who is observing the dream cannot read them. And though the I who is in the dream commences to speak them out loud, the I who is observing the dream cannot hear them. There is no more poet's hand, no more poet's hair, there is no longer any poet. There are only the words on the page, the sound of the words spoken in my own voice, and the impossibility of ever knowing what they are—

SUBPLOT RISING

quickly as a bird
or early as a baby
slowly as a veil
as often as a blush

CONFESSIONAL

Overhearing myself cough I become aware that despite all
my urgent efforts, I have failed at honesty. Why is this?

Is it because the self, unable to fully see itself, is unable
to represent itself? I so wish to conclude my verse novel,

yet continue to note arbitrary details of my surroundings;
the sexual happiness of the couple on the couch, his ex-

tremely long fingers. After the movie in which
the protagonist mistakenly murders his wife,

I lay my head on my husband's chest,
struck with terror and regret. How poorly

I have loved him. How soon we
both will die. He, characteristically,

shifts under the weight of my head, "Get off.
You're hurting me," & stands

to put the dishes in the sink. I go
to check the status of our baby's breath.

She breathes. It's the last sound I'm
aware of before I sleep to dream

another chapter in this, my fidelity.
Conclusion: It is briefly possible

for a bird in the air to take the place

of a woman's head.

TEARS: SUBPLOT WELLING

That was because

   an eye that is

      like an insect, never still,

sliding and sliding behind a glass

     lens

will slowly, very, very slowly,

     bury itself.

59

Take off your clothes, he said. When she didn't, he stuck his elbow between her ribs. Shrieking laughter—what once had seemed vehemence now seemed to shiver like asphalt under extreme heat. Are you inviting me to the movies, she asked when freed? The test would be if you could see your own child standing in a doorway facing a yellow field blown by a hard wind and not bend down to turn him around. I began to take walks in the park. "Seeing myself" as a way to prepare for transformation. Down, down, down the arm comes, glistening in the sun like a slowed blade. Soundless, the only lit thing, without target or initiation. Imagine ice moving over water, sent by a current of invisible source. It slides, seemingly for no cause. And now the sound: a cracking like thunder, then deep melodramatic rumble. And surprisingly, there are goats in the park, strewn all over the hill like daisies. And a spectacle of reassurance emerges in the shape of a man and a woman, each with a child riding piggyback. It was then I began to notice the repetitions in the scene: bump, bump, then *green:* bump, bump, then *green*. Over and over, a kind of rhythmic stubbornness, that, rocking us, like an echo does, let us sleep again, surrounded by cushions of intermittent fulfillment. Lively and intact the time of day
settled in the green and was sent—

WHAT IS "TO CARRY"

And placed the teabags and bread on the table, their weight lasting a certain long time. Then giving up. Must as an absolute demand and will. Do. But one time I turned to lift and found like Alice I was holding what I had not meant. The light, then, as a crisis of knowledge. I couldn't but clasp it but became weary of its unrest.

SUBPLOT IN QUICK REVERSE

Pause—must we then? You might like to lock the door, for your teacher's mind is on display. Adieu, adieu! (they laugh). And your job is to warn me, the jovial twin in a fold of linen. Fast cry.

61

If a crow sits on the skull of a deer that's the

end.

The middle is marked by

rising tides, fountains,

wings.

The beginning was

a series of interruptions

that fell into the shape

of a problem.

—

Of three readers reading, one favors the end,

reads for a solution, a settling of wings,

reads for a death, or death's foreboding.

The second reader only
                rereads the beginning;

all purchase, all perch—never to arrive.

This reader's thrust

      into steady anxiety, made bearable by

                its partner, curiosity—

             still, it is difficult to breathe.

The third reader reading does not move at all.

      Enraptured—she is entirely

of the middle made.

      The problem, its solution,

they hold no importance; she bathes

        in water unbound, unbroken.

Reading neither

forward nor backward

she hovers in the midst. And yet,

each sentence, each word,
hides its own dark finitude—

And in choosing never to resolve

never not to,
she must eventually

dispense with

all—

THE OUTSIDE DEMANDS;
THE INSIDE DELIVERS

What is "transition"

Always at this hour, "Good God, it's over," then the argument
extends into a circle. The clouds are dark, that's what the challenge
is, dark as the ballast of breath. Transition is a body of water they
named shame because they were afraid to cross it. Transition is a
door in the movement of time we call beat or pulse, we call meter.
I am here, I said over and over, my voice fading.

What is the "matter"

First the woman's back appeared painted as a scene of eating. Then
the image went and was replaced by the sensation of being
watched. She stayed very still under the gaze of the thousand eyes.
Sleepless. Matter gives birth to more of the same, but the laughter
was loud and distracted us from completing our plan. I was angry
and hit the board, saying no more, as evenly I was kissed by a
calling.

What is "ring"

With a crack down the middle the bell could not again. Held by
its holding it solders as a circle. A ring around the eye, in the tree,
in the mouth. A crack down the middle and you must rip it open.
Let her love him, she'll not speak to him. Sold, not yet enjoyed,
her shame stutters.

What is "color"

It rises. It comes between. It's a parallel strain once the music's turned off. I had crayons and a book in a box and offered them to the bored little girls. They jumped at the offer. The girls were a color and they were dismayed when the book was already colored. And looked up at me. What do we do now?

What is "the end"

It lingers in the face. Liquid contralto. It lingers in the memory of its arrival. In the swelling of tones, the quickening of plot, in the third repetition. Especially in the third repetition. His hair spreads on the pillow. He turns on the engine then gets out of it. The end is a false translation of the present. And yet the wall was studded with signs.

SUBPLOT RESOLVES, FADING

They walk on a rug above the ground
floor, they walk on only
when called upon to speak.
And they lie down at once
in the overblown wind,
then swim in a puddle of runoff.

They fold the sheet to hide in its folds

while laughing again in their mouths . . .

63

He reads: Rain-dark clouds. Staying married. Says,
not lost to
wet fields and photographs
of snow, the end. It was and it wasn't. Is and isn't.
The boy saying, c'mon Mom let's take a walk. There's
nowhere to go, she answers. She serves eggs on bits of
paper and balances her hair. Swept,
the floor could
never be, never clean, I was and wasn't
mixed into the various. Both alone (mountain) and
multiplied (mountain) I rolled backward through
water. Friends given over to ambition, grief, or bad news
didn't call. I was always missing but nearly,
my mind was wet. I'd forgotten how to blush, left
dear flushed face in the fallen grasses reading:

When he gives me a light he has to—

walking home from returning we

decide to open a press

it sleeps I am to

wake it watched

by the eyes of a god he ascends

the stairs in search of *I*

pretended to be a monster explains the flattened the water

moves us not the other way around breaking

upon the stones was

a thousand stones

breaking

a thousand stones

upon the stones the water

moves us not the other way

around breaking I *pretended to be a monster*

explains the flattened stairs

in search of

the yes of a god he ascends

wake it watched it sleeps

I am to decide to open to press

walking home from returning we

One is urged to step back for a

broader view

and one asks to be so viewed.

Largely having forgotten my hand

I turned to my face and was spent.

A portrait met another one

but there was no ground on which to stand so they knelt.

Fear took the form of falling snow

while the aged in the water barely moved.

The body widened and asked to be forgotten

just as groundless fear fell as show.

Hands in the face and later

the pool,

until largely having turned, they were blessed.

NOTES

Epigraph: Emily Dickinson #451.

Epigraph: Anne Carson, *Men in the Off Hours* (New York: Knopf, 2000), 130.

Section 2: "The tree like a valve of the heart opens in the open sun" is a rewording of a line from Cole Swensen's "Nine Trees" in *Noon* (Los Angeles: Sun & Moon, 1997), 28.

Section 5: "the enclasping flow" is from Matthew Arnold's "To Marguerite—Continued":

> Yes; in the sea of life enisl'd
> With echoing straits between us thrown
> Dotting the shoreless watery wild
> We mortal millions live *alone*
> The islands feel the enclasping flow,
> And then their endless bounds they know.

Section 8: Language throughout this section and the other sections of the same title, 17 and 62, is inspired by Juliet's speeches in *Romeo and Juliet*, Act I, scene iii; II. ii; and III. ii. Juliet's second line, spoken to her mother is, "Madam, I am here."

Subplot 1: This text misquotes a passage from *The Memoirs of John Addington Symonds: The Secret Homosexual Life of a Leading Nineteenth-Century Man of Letters*, ed. Phyllis Grosskurth (Chicago: University of Chicago Press, 1984), 99.

Section 19: "The self is a servant only / To its source" is from Fanny Howe's *Selected Poems* (Berkeley: University of California Press, 2000), 101.

Section 28: This text is directly derived from Edmund Spenser's "Epithalamion" in that most of the language is his and is incorporated by following his poem's sequence.

Section 34: The tapestry described, by Leonardo Drew, is titled *#24* and hangs in the Metropolitan Museum of Art in New York.

Section 35: The flush left text is from Rilke's "Woman in Love," slightly rearranged, in *New Poems: The Other Part*, trans. Edward Snow (Berkeley: North Point Press, 1987), 169.

Section 36: Some lines and sentiment borrowed (but adulterated) from Matthew Arnold's "Dover Beach."

Section 40: This poem borrows its main idea from a poem entitled "Twin," by Shira Dentz, published in the web journal *How2*, Fall 2003.

Section 44: Text throughout is borrowed from Matthew Arnold's "To Marguerite—continued" and "Dover Beach."

Section 53: This text is derived from a failed download of Gerard Manley Hopkins's "Epithalamion," a poem considered to be unfinished.

Section 63: The italicized line is from "Renting a Room" by Sarah Kirsch, translated by Wayne Kvam, and found in *Poems for the Millennium: The University of California Book of Modern and Postmodern Poetry*, vol. 2, ed. Jerome Rothenberg and Pierre Joris (Berkeley: University of California Press, 1998).

ACKNOWLEDGMENTS

Grateful acknowledgement is made to the editors of the following journals in which some of these poems have appeared: *American Letters and Commentary* ("44. How He Stands, Close Enough"); *Lit* ("36," "49. The Outside lamented by the Inside"); *Pool* ("6. Doing," "13"); *The Canary* ("47. Five Portraits in Rings [Sentences with Objects]"); *Tarpaulin Sky*, a web journal ("16. Five Sentences with Nouns," "28. Epithalamion: Spencer [echo ring]," "Subplot 3," "30. Fire," "39. Six Sentences with and without Adjectives [portraits in Boxes]," "63," "Subplot descending"); *3rd Bed* ("27. Three Sentences with Adverbs," "32. Water/Fire [for the baby]," "50. Six Sentences Darkly with Nouns Spent," "51. The Same Six Sentences Revised," "Tears: Subplot Welling," "62. The Outside Demands: the Inside Delivers"); *Xantippe* ("1," "2," "10. The Outside Observes the Inside Again," "34. Tapestry: A Metaphor," "45. Fourth Part Broken").

Thank you to Laynie Browne, Shira Dentz, Jessica Fisher, Anna Grace, Lyn Hejinian, Sharon Krauss, Heather McHugh, Reginald Shepherd, and Brian Teare for friendship, guidance, and support, and for enormously insightful readings of this work. My gratitude also to Carlos Ferguson for the use of his artwork. Thanks to the University of California, Berkeley, English Department for general good spirit and encouragement. Thanks especially and always to Tim Roberts for collaborations both of and off the page.

THE CONTEMPORARY POETRY SERIES
Edited by Paul Zimmer

THE CONTEMPORARY POETRY SERIES
Edited by Bin Ramke